DARE TO WRITE

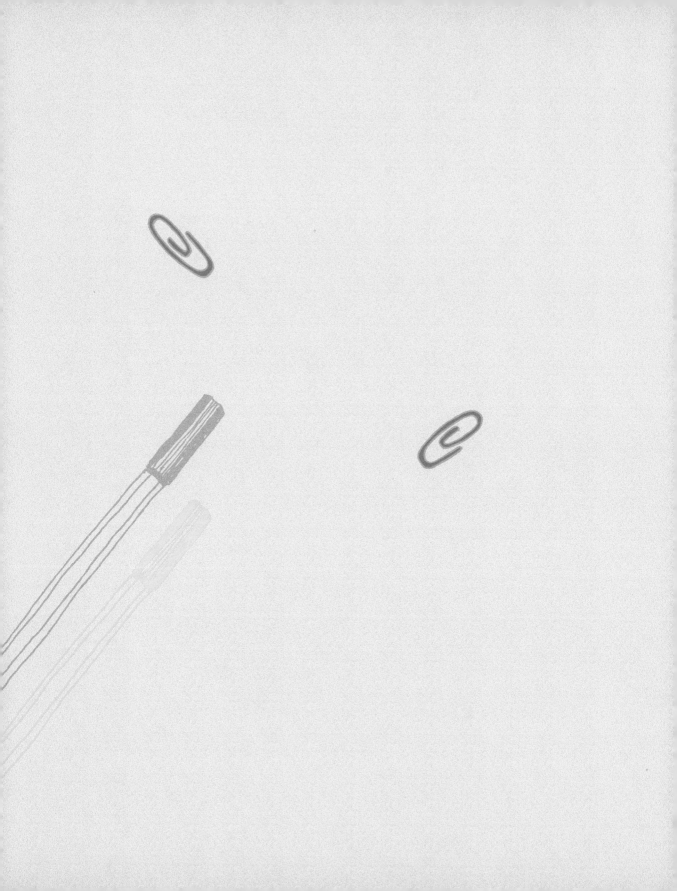

DARE *to* WRITE

Creative Writing Prompts

FOR YOUNG PEOPLE
AND WORD REBELS
EVERYWHERE

KRISTEN FOGLE

ROCKRIDGE
PRESS

Interior and Cover Designer: Erin Yeung
Art Producer: Sue Bischofberger
Editor: Rochelle Torke
Production Manager: Riley Hoffman
Production Editor: Melissa Edeburn

Illustration courtesy of Creative Market and Shutterstock.

ISBN: Print 978-1-64152-870-2 | eBook 978-1-64152-924-2

FOR MOM, WHO ALWAYS PROMPTED ME TO FOLLOW MY DREAMS.

Contents

Introduction

Hi, I'm Kristen. I run a writing center called San Diego Writers, Ink.

But way before that, I started penning epically embarrassing journal entries in the second grade. I went on to write a lot of short stories—even a horror story starring my eighth-grade class—and a terrible "Ask Dr. Love" column for my high school newspaper. All that writing fed my passion for the craft. Now I get to help others work on their own stories every day.

One thing I love about my work, aside from creating cool programs for writers, is leading prompt-powered writing groups. We get together and use words and story starts like the ones you'll find in this book to help our imaginations take us in surprising directions.

With the right prompt, your wild and frisky brain can venture any-where. A good prompt can ignite a poem, free a trapped novel, trigger a cathartic brain dump, let a singed heart speak, or simply give you space to rant about the burnt pizza, if that's what you need to do.

I'M SO GLAD YOU'RE HERE

When it comes to chasing our creative sparks, there's no destination and no wrong way to dive in and start writing.

Perhaps you picked up this book because you already love to write. Or maybe it was a gift from your aunt, and you don't know yet what to think. Either way, I'm happy you're here.

So, let's get started. Here's your invitation to take the plunge, play around, and get to know your own unique, incredibly creative mind.

HOW TO USE THIS BOOK

This book is organized by genre and you can dive in anywhere you like. I suggest you start with chapter 1: Writing Workshop (page 1) because it offers some reminders and writerly resources that might help you have even more fun as you roam around the book. You'll also notice some craft tips scattered throughout, just to help you try new tricks.

Lastly, there's lots of space to write in the book—if that's your thing. Or, if you really get going with a new story, you may want to use a notebook instead. However you decide to use it, this book is yours now, so do with it what you will. I hope you come back to it whenever you're stuck or just want to have some fun.

CHAPTER 1

Writing Workshop

Writing is a bit like making a great dinner. You could wing it, go crazy in the kitchen, and turn out something delicious. But having a little knowledge about your ingredients and how to put them together usually leads to the tastiest results. It's the same with writing.

In this chapter, we'll talk about the craft of writing—like how to use characters, setting, dialogue, and conflict to build a story. These are classic ingredients of zesty, crunchy, mouthwatering, back-for-seconds writing.

So what are you waiting for? Grab a fork—I mean, a pen—and dive in.

CHARACTERS

Compelling characters pull readers into your story. So it's important to spend time crafting them.

One starting point is to think about what your character wants. The most compelling characters are driven by desire—all kinds of wants, needs, and motivations. Now think about a character you'd like to write about. What does he want? What's her burning wish? Does she long to win a pumpkin contest in Iowa or colonize an asteroid? Whatever your characters are after, desire makes them real and interesting to your reader.

Next, think about their physical appearance or other traits. For instance, let's say I had a character who wanted to rob a bank. I might describe his facial expressions or mannerisms like this: His eyes darted back and forth. If I wanted to reveal that my character was quirky, I might turn to her style of dress: She wore a patchwork vest, a short, striped top, and bright orange tights.

Building characters is a fun part of honing your writing skills. This book will help you do just that.

Your Turn

PLUCK A CHARACTER FROM THE WORLD AROUND YOU

Go to a library, a public park, or anywhere with a lot of foot traffic. Notice people: their clothing and movement and where they seem to be going. Borrow inspiration from them. Let their qualities influence your characters. See someone with an unusual way of moving? Maybe you spy someone who has an exaggerated mannerism, like a huge laugh or an explosive cough. Write about the qualities you see.

BUILD A CHARACTER BY ANSWERING QUESTIONS:

The most important things that have happened to my character are:

....

....

....

My character's favorite outfit is:

....

....

....

The values my character lives by are:

....

....

....

My character would never:

....

....

....

....

....

My character dreams of:

....

....

....

....

....

My character's friends would describe my character as:

....

....

....

....

....

One of my character's quirks is:

....

....

....

....

....

When nervous, my character:

....
....
....
....
....

My character's daily routine includes:

....
....
....
....
....

When speaking, my character sounds like:

....
....
....
....
....

My character is a little bit like these movie characters:

....
....
....
....
....

HOW SETTING BUILDS STORY

Setting will do many great things for your writing. Yes, it's the geographic location of your tale but it is also the era in history, the season, and even the time of day when your story takes place. Because setting can build the mood for your story, it's great to introduce it at the beginning.

To do this, we have to give details, all at once or a bit at a time. Also, appeal to the senses—we want to be able to *taste* the biscuits in the cafe and *smell* the coffee just as much as we want to *see* the long line of desperate, undercaffeinated customers or the clueless but charming barista behind the bar.

Here are three examples of details that paint the scene:

- Given the house full of candelabras, chandeliers, and pearl-encrusted everything, it was obvious that she was rich.

- The school contained nothing but broken erasers, dusty chalkboards, and dirty children.

- The inn always smelled of disinfectant and detergent, which wafted through every tucked sheet and precisely folded towel.

Your Turn

READY, SET, SETTING!

Here's a prompt to get you started if you already have a setting in mind:

Set a timer. Close your eyes. Spend a few minutes imagining a fictional room surrounding you, visualizing your setting. Take in every detail. Consider what your character feels about this place, too. Then, after the time is up, write all the adjectives and phrases that come to mind as quickly as you can. Edit later—just write! Borrow what you came up with here if you get stumped describing your setting later.

Go on then

PAINT THE SCENE

Here are a few more jumping-off points to help you flesh out a new story setting:

Describe the first place you ever lived or somewhere that was magical to you when you were younger.

You're in a large hotel ballroom on election night and your candidate has won. Discuss the decor, the people, the mood, and the feeling in the room.

The bus back home always smells like . . .

You've been miniaturized. Someone has stuck your mini-self in the drawer next to your bed. Detail the ordinary items you encounter, their size, and what it's like to see them from your new, tiny vantage point.

Imagine you're in a cemetery. What do you hear? What do you experience through your other senses?

Your character has been captured. While peering through the edge of the blindfold, they notice these 10 things about their surroundings. What are they?

Describe a doctor's office in the 1900s through the eyes of a patient who's going to have a major procedure.

Go further: Imagine the same office in the 2100s. What has changed?

DIALOGUE TOOLS

What your characters say and how they say it is another powerful element in spinning a good yarn—and it's another way to keep readers hooked. Remember that dialogue should:

1. Advance the plot. That means it should carry your story forward, revealing conflicts or new directions for the narrative. Here's an example:

    > "So you actually saw her at the scene of the crime."
    > "I know you won't tell anyone."
    > "You're crazy. Then again, I don't deal with cops."

2. Give insight into a character's motivations or the way they're viewed by other characters, like this back-and-forth:

    > "Why did you vote no on that bill?"
    > "Maybe I don't believe in it."
    > "You don't know what you believe anymore. The only thing you care about is what Jack thinks."
    > "You don't know anything."
    > "That's what it's always about. Jack, Jack, Jack."

3. Give insight into your character's relationship with another character.

    > "You always treat people like they're less than you."
    > "That's ridiculous. Get out of my way."

Your Turn

Use these dialogue starters and keep the conversation going:

1. Character A: "Great, now Mom knows we snuck out."

   Character B: "She wouldn't have found out if you hadn't told everyone at school."

2. Character A: "You're firing me?"

   Character B: "You're a thief. Just because we're friends doesn't mean I can let this go!"

3. Character A: "I was hoping we could talk about you and me."

   Character B: "What is there to say? You were the one who dumped me."

4. Character A: "I don't want to make you nervous, but I hear something."

   Character B: "Do you think one of them escaped?"

So they said

So they said

BONUS! ACT IT OUT.

Try this: Get a friend and act out a scene in character together while recording it on your phone. Then swap roles. How does hearing the words said out loud change your dialogue writing style?

KEEPIN' IT REAL

How do we get our characters to sound like real people? The right details help your characters live and breathe. Here are a few things to consider when you want your characters to sound legit:

Occupational slang: Does your character have a way of speaking related to their profession? For instance, a doctor and a plumber might use different vocabulary related to their trade.

Accents and dialects: A Southerner might slip in a "y'all" every now and again, whereas a Californian might unknowingly pepper their speech with "like."

Personality: How does your character's mood and personality come through in your dialogue? Does the character use fewer words because they're shy or afraid? A bold and gossipy character may have a lot to say, or might interrupt other characters.

JUST ADD TROUBLE

Conflict, stalled plans, thwarted dreams, deflected ambitions—tension of all shapes and sizes is the catalyzing energy of an interesting story. It's what keeps us wondering what will happen. We *enjoy* watching characters pass tests or solve problems. Imagine what *The Three Little Pigs* would be without that pesky wolf.

But because sometimes that's easier said than done, the table below can help you. I've filled out a few conflict ideas you can borrow from; feel free to mix and match.

Your Turn

Mix and match these characters, desires, and roadblocks.

CHARACTER	DESIRE	ROADBLOCK
A politician	To change the world	They were born into a famous crime family
A small-town teen	To find love	Their mother expects obedience and conformity
A poet	Fame	Crippling shyness
A high school quarterback	To come out of the closet	A secret phobia

More trouble, more story

ADDING SPICE WITH FRESH LANGUAGE

Fresh, fun language helps readers savor your story. Here are some tips for choosing sharp, specific words that evoke the setting, emotions, or other crucial details of your tale:

1. Be specific: "He threw *trash* at the bully" could become more vivid and visual this way: "He hurled *a soda can* at the bully's face."
2. Consider nixing words that repeat the same idea: "The teacher had a rule about *injuring or wounding* anyone."
3. Borrow from poetry—rhythm, rhyme, and alliteration are your friends: "The pitter-patter of rain calmed the kitten."
4. Replace common verbs like "was" with something more descriptive. Instead of writing "She was late," conjure an image: "She darted in, hair a mess, three minutes after the bell."

Your Turn

Keep a word diary for a few days. Write down any snippets of conversations you hear that might make good dialogue. Capture words that are new to you or pleasing to the ear. Collect these words and snippets to include in your stories whenever you're in need.

Captured here

CHAPTER 2

According to Me
(Memoir and Self-Inquiry Prompts)

A memoir is simply writing about something that has happened to you. It doesn't have to be the story of your whole existence. It's just a collection of memories or reflections from a period of your life or a particular situation. You can borrow from your experiences and share them on the page.

Memoir can also be fun because these stories are your own and you can tell them any way you like. The following prompts will help you write about yourself. They may also make you feel a bit exposed. Fear not—these exercises are about flexing your writing muscles. It's up to you whether anyone ever reads them.

STUFF THAT HAPPENED TO ME

I've found that the best writers know themselves. A great way to discover more about yourself is to put your thoughts, beliefs, and experiences into writing.

Experienced memoir writers like Joan Didion and David Sedaris are able to dial into their experiences and are mindful of their true emotions. As a result, they create memorable accounts and deeply relatable experiences that connect with all kinds of readers.

The easiest part about memoir is that you don't need to make anything up. Everything comes from your life. In this exercise, we'll churn up some memories and help you dive right into your personal trove of story fodder.

Your Turn

Dare yourself to explore one (or many) of *your* real-life plot points by trying one of these:

What do your mementos tell you? Try this: Grab some items that mean a lot to you. Close your eyes and pick an item. Write for 10 minutes on the story, event, or person the object reminds you of.

....

....

....

....

....

....

When in your life were you genuinely surprised?

....

....

....

Write about a major change you've experienced—either your own or someone else's that affected you. Perhaps focus on a new friendship or talk about the time you switched schools.

....

....

....

My favorite pet taught me about . . .

....

....

....

Day in the life: Where were you a decade ago? Imagine what you may have been doing on this day exactly 10 years in the past.

....

....

....

A time I felt truly talented was . . .

....

....

....

What were you like as a baby? Interview someone who knows.

....

....

....

The trip I'll never forget is . . .

....

....

....

Pick a teacher. What important lesson did you learn from this teacher?

....

....

....

The best you've ever felt. When was it? What happened?

....

....

....

The most major event in history that I've been alive for is probably . . .

....

....

....

....

Talk about the most important test you have ever taken or will take.

....
....
....

Write about one thing you wish you could forget.

....
....
....

The book that changed my life was . . .

....
....
....

If our family had a secret, it would be . . .

....
....
....

Everything changed the day I met . . .

....
....
....

Write about the biggest fight you ever had.

....

....

....

....

This seemingly unimportant event made all the difference because . . .

....

....

....

....

I would be a totally different person if _____ hadn't happened.

....

....

....

....

What topic do I write about most? Why?

....

....

....

....

MY DREAMS

Let's hear them. Understanding and writing about your dreams is a great way to understand yourself. Plus, you'll flex the same writing muscles and investigative tools that you need to write about other people—real or fictional ones.

Your Turn

Ask yourself these questions and don't be afraid to write the truth.

What is your ideal boyfriend or girlfriend like?

....

....

....

Is love at first sight real?

....

....

....

The last dream I remember is . . .

....

....

....

The job I don't want is . . .

....

....

....

When I reach (age)_____, I will live like . . .

....

....

....

I most want to learn about . . .

....

....

....

If I could become the best at something, what would it be?

....

....

....

Is luck or hard work more important? Write about a time something happened to you due to either luck or hard work.

....

....

....

What are the top five countries you want to visit?

....

....

....

What's the last place you'd ever visit?

....

....

....

Write about a time you were ambitious . . . and it didn't pay off.

....

....

....

How important is fame?

....

....

....

If you believe in fate, what does yours look like?

....

....

....

Are you more passionate or more curious? Describe a time you were one of the two.

....
....
....
....
....

If you could devote your life to one cause, what would it be?

....
....
....
....
....

If you could erase one thing from the world with a snap of your fingers, what would it be?

....
....
....
....
....

WHAT FREAKS ME OUT

What makes you squeamish or scared? Let's also look at your past and the scary things you overcame—because not all stories are warm and fuzzy.

Your Turn

Don't let a little thing like fear push you around. Writing how you really feel and what you really think can be a load off.

I am at my worst when I . . .

....
....
....

When I'm scared, it tastes like . . .

....
....
....

The riskiest thing I have done is . . .

....
....
....

Talk about a time when fear was necessary.

....
....
....

I'm afraid of people who . . .

....
....
....

What happened the last time you were rejected?

....
....
....

When I'm nervous, it looks like . . .

....
....
....

Describe the most terrifying animal you've ever seen.

....
....
....

What's worse—getting older or giving a presentation in front of a lot of people?

....
....
....
....
....
....

What's scarier, standing at the top of a tall building or being stuck in an enclosed space?

....
....
....
....
....
....

If you were dropped onto a desolate island alone, what one tool would you take with you?

....
....
....
....
....
....

A nightmare I had recently is . . .

....
....
....
....
....
....

Write about a time you were brave.

....
....
....
....
....
....

The food I don't understand why people eat is . . .

....
....
....
....
....
....

I TAKE IT BACK (REGRETS)

Face it: Our regrets teach us a lot about ourselves. So take a big breath and get comfortable, because these things are not easy to write about. But just as you wouldn't judge a character too harshly, don't be too hard on yourself.

Your Turn

Do tell.

Have you ever stolen anything?

....

....

....

....

The thing I am most jealous of is . . .

....

....

....

My parents said no but I . . .

....

....

....

What does disappointment sound like?

....

....

....

When you're 80 years old, looking back on your life, what could you imagine you might be remorseful about?

....

....

....

Describe something you might find funny even though you know it's not polite or moral.

....

....

....

Is guilt ever useful?

....

....

....

What would your best friend say is your biggest regret? What would your family say?

....

....

....

What does a missed opportunity sound like?

....

....

....

....

Write about a time you almost made a costly mistake.

....

....

....

....

What have you covered up? What do you wish you could cover up?

....

....

....

....

When you were a kid, what did you think the worst rule to break was? Did you break it?

....

....

....

....

I BELIEVE

This exercise is about finding out what you stand for. The answers to these questions might surprise you.

Your Turn

What do you really think? Remember that you can share these answers with others—or take them to your grave. You can also revisit your responses in six months or six years to see how your opinions have changed.

Is there ever a good reason to lie?

....
....
....

How do you feel about the death penalty?

....
....
....

How has religion changed your life for better or worse?

....
....
....

What is the best gift you could receive?

....

....

....

Is poverty or discrimination a bigger problem?

....

....

....

What's the best way to win an argument?

....

....

....

What is the most important thing that people younger than you need
to understand about teenagers? What about people older than you?

....

....

....

Which is more important: travel or education?

....

....

....

What movie does your life resemble, or what movie do you *wish* your life resembled?

....
....
....
....

Can love conquer all?

....
....
....
....

Who is one of your muses or mentors? Why?

....
....
....
....

When people say "money can't buy happiness," do you believe them?

....
....
....
....

MY LIFE IN COMEDY

These prompts might ask you to step out of your comfort zone. Not all of them are cool, but you should do them anyway because they'll tell you something about yourself.

Your Turn

Jot down one of these story starts and see what happens.

1. The weirdest thing I've ever seen is . . .
2. If I could have one absurd superpower, it would be . . .
3. An embarrassing thing I lived through is . . .
4. Describe your worst Halloween costume. Now the best one.
5. Write a stand-up comedy routine about your day.
6. You get to switch places with someone for the day. Write about that experience.
7. If it came to life, the inanimate object that I would definitely be friends with would be . . .
8. Imagine you had to enter an eating contest, but you could choose the food—what would it be?
9. The most ridiculous habit I have is . . .
10. I secretly find _____ entertaining.
11. Create a new recipe—except don't use food. For example, a salad made out of clothing.
12. A famous dancer is going to pay you a ton of money to choreograph your happy dance. Describe the dance. Where is the best place to perform it? Who should be at the performance? Who shouldn't?

PROMPT # _____

PROMPT # _____

PROMPT # _____

PROMPT # _____

PROMPT # _____

PROMPT # _____

PROMPT # _____

SHOW DON'T TELL

When you *tell*, you're giving the audience information directly, like:

- She was tired.

- He hated school.

- They were not friends.

Showing is about using feelings, actions, and description instead of just handing over the facts. Showing lets the reader use their imagination to connect the dots. Let's practice: Instead of saying that your character is hard of hearing, for instance, you might say that "he cupped his ear, trying to patch together enough sounds to follow the conversation." Instead of mentioning that a child is excited, you could describe how she clutches at her mother's dress, jumps up and down, and makes shrill noises.

Here's another example:

Telling the reader: Tom hated the hot weather.

Showing the reader: Tom's insides turned crimson and his stomach lurched. The July sun was pitiless on his pale skin.

Your Turn

Look for a few "tell" sentences you may have already written in your notebook. Play around with revising these to "show" the reader instead.

So they said

CHAPTER 3

Crimes, Misdemeanors, and Total Mysteries

Kidnapping, arson, imprisonment—this section is rife with intrigue and conflict. Whether you're writing from the perspective of a well-meaning sleuth or a cold-blooded criminal, here I invite you to flesh out your protagonist with a character worksheet. Feel free to invent as many characters as you like with this worksheet technique and use your creations as you play around with the prompts in this chapter.

CHARACTER WORKSHEET

Name:	Occupation:
Gender:	Age:
Physical description:	Personality description:
Dwelling place:	Skills:
Crimes already committed:	Reasons for committing crimes:
Strengths:	Weaknesses:
Backstory (what else do we need to know about this character?):	What does this character want right now?
What stands in their way?	What might cause them to turn their life around?

AND ACTION!

I invite you to keep cooking up complex criminals, misunderstood villains, and heroic (or corrupt) detectives. Whoever is rattling around in your imagination at the moment, let's see them in action using the prompts below.

Your Turn

Let these story starts take you anyplace you'd like to go.

Stealing the statue had been easy . . . too easy. The booming knock at the door tells him his luck might be running out.

When he wakes up, his hands are tied behind his back and he is in the back of a van. The rear door is ajar, so he . . .

Years ago, she had found the ancient key with the Greek letters Εξκγ engraved on the side. Walking home from school, she spies an abandoned house with the same carving over the doorway, so she . . .

Your character's brother has started sleepwalking. Every morning, at 3:13 a.m., he walks down the stairs, unlocks the deadbolt, and ventures outside. Tonight, when your character follows him, she . . .

On television, your character overhears the newscaster talking about a murder scene, where the only clue left behind is a rare _____. She realizes she's seen _____ before—at her best friend's house. Your character decides to . . .

She has been stopped for speeding on the freeway. She's had a perfect driving record until now, so she isn't worried. But the officer looks at her license and says, "Step out of the car, miss, we've been looking for you."

STORY STARTS, GAMES, AND OTHER PROMPTS

Here are some writing games to help you kick off your next mystery or thriller. Remember, you can include the characters you cooked up using the preceding worksheet—or take off with a fresh idea.

Your Turn

Grab a prompt and let the story begin.

1. Describe what happened at the hypnotist's show.

2. She didn't start the fire. But she knew who did.

3. The crime he almost got away with . . .

4. He claims she was falsely imprisoned. Here's what really happened.

5. Write about the disappearance that changed the town forever.

6. The private detective always carries five useful tools. They are . . .

7. This is the smell that solved the mystery.

8. Write down all the words that come to mind when you hear the word "psychic."

9. The deserted cave was silent until they heard . . .

10. You wake up in a room you've never seen before. The first thing you do is . . .

11. Retell the ghost story that scares you most. Bonus: Create a new ending.

12. She loved puzzles. But when she put this one together, the word _____ was spelled out.

13. This is where the map told him to go.

14. Your character saw who vandalized the school that night. What does he do?

15. Start a story that begins with one of these words: shuddering, creaking, dissecting, mortuary, disturbance. Bonus: Keep adding a new word from this list to your writing every two to three minutes.

PROMPT # _____

PROMPT # _____

PROMPT # _____

PROMPT # _____

PROMPT # _____

PROMPT # _____

PROMPT # _____

PROMPT # _____

PROMPT # _____

PROMPT # _____

PORTRAIT OF A PERSON, PLACE, OR THING—RAPID-FIRE!

Let's put your writing skills to work—with a little time pressure. Give yourself just three minutes to write about the following person, place, or thing.

Your Turn

Pick a phrase and see what your beautiful brain wants to do with it.

A gravestone with a word scratched out	A stranger crying
An unexplained stench	Stealing someone's boyfriend

Someone stealing from you

An empty circus tent

An unlocked safe

The secret society

A hitchhiker who turns out not
to be a stranger

Gunshots

A recurring dream

When a missing friend reappears after
10 years

The last thing they expected to find was a coffin

A box of memories—and a confession

The abandoned house with dishes on the table

The high-security government building on the edge of town

More to say?

WHO'S TELLING THE STORY?

There are several points of view (POV) that you could use to write a story. I invite you to test-drive the four narrative voices below as you start new stories. But wait, what's a narrative voice? In writing, the narrator is the voice telling the story. When you write a memoir, the author is the narrator. When you write fiction, the narrator could be any one of these:

First person. The narrator is also a character in the story. First-person stories use "I" or "we." Imagine a story where the main character, an archaeologist, is also the one telling the story. Example: "At last, we uncovered the stone and saw the carved message."

Second person. The reader becomes the character and "you" is used. Example: "You survey the burnt remains of the theater, your mind racing." Writing fiction in the second person is a bit uncommon and can be really fun to experiment with.

Third person limited. The narrator is not a character in the story but has information about the main character (including access to their internal thoughts). "He," "she," and "they" are used. Example: "He thought about her all day but doubted she even knew his name."

Third person omniscient. As with third person limited, this narrative voice uses "he," "she," and "they," but the storyteller has access to everyone's thoughts and feelings. "Like all the villagers, Malcolm feared dragons and usually avoided the forest. His mother was proud of her obedient son and would have been horrified if she knew what he was really plotting." Here, the narrator can explain the beliefs of any character. Omniscient narration was popular in folk stories and fairy tales, but some modern authors have enjoyed success with it as well.

Your Turn

Pick a paragraph from your writing that's told in one point of view and rewrite it in a different point of view. Notice how sometimes a shift in perspective can transform a story—and send your writerly imagination in a whole new direction.

So they said

Go on then

CHAPTER 4

Don't You Love Love?

Love stories come in all shapes, sizes, and heartache levels. But even if you want to pen a syrupy romance, remember that a story is a story. That means it needs action, conflict, motives, and interesting characters. I invite you to pepper your romantic story with chaos, upheavals, obstacles, and inconvenient love triangles.

Even in the love genre, most compelling stories are full of problems. In this section, please use the next character worksheet to create a pair of people in a relationship. You can then include them in the exercises that follow.

CHARACTER WORKSHEET

Names:	Occupations:
Genders:	Ages:
Physical descriptions:	Personality descriptions:
Dwelling:	Backstory (what else do we need to know about these characters?):
Strengths:	Weaknesses:
Who do these characters love and why?	What stands between these characters and the person they love?

AND ACTION!

Now that you've crafted your ill-fated lovebirds, put them into action by using the prompts below. Choose a path and finish the story.

Your Turn

Choose your adventure with these phrases and situations.

She felt sick to her stomach when she saw. . .

- his arm wrapped around someone she'd never seen before.
- the diamond engagement ring in his drawer.
- his photo on an ID with a different name.

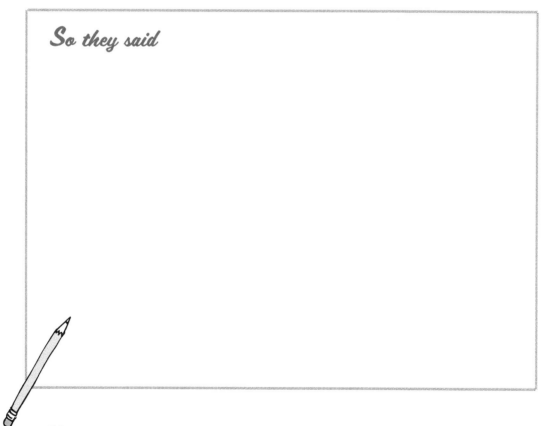

So they said

She gasped when . . .

- he led her to a field with a blanket and picnic basket.
- she saw her ex-boyfriend outside her car window.
- she realized she had sent a romantic text to the wrong person.

Try it

He felt his blood boil when he found out . . .

- his crush had abandoned him at the dance.
- his ex-girlfriend had spread a lie about him.
- his sister told his crush he had an illness.

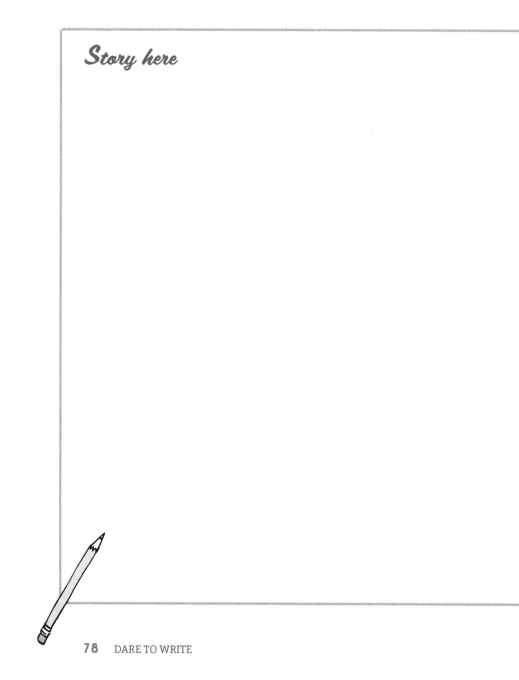

Story here

While speed dating, he was surprised to run into . . .

- the girl he'd been trying to talk to all year long.
- his ex-boyfriend.
- his mom!

What do you say?

The couple was shocked when . . .

- they found an old man smoking a cigar in the cabin they'd rented for the weekend.
- they came home to find their wedding invitations torn up on the floor.
- one of their mothers told them they could never be together.

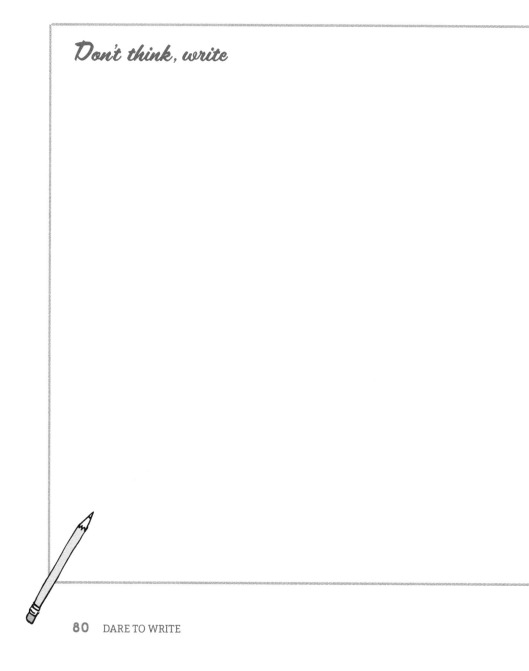

Don't think, write

Beside his yearbook photo, he wrote to her . . .

- "Meet me by the flagpole after school on the last day. I have to tell you something."
- "I'm sorry . . . I respect you . . . but I don't feel the same."
- "I made a mistake when I didn't ask you out."

The story begins

STORY STARTS, GAMES, AND OTHER PROMPTS

Here are some writing games to get your next tale started. Remember, you can use the characters from the worksheet to build out the prompts here.

Your Turn

Grab a prompt and go, Cupid.

1. Start a story that begins with one of these words: roller coaster, harsh, letter, lingering, glance, glare, or dance. Bonus: Keep adding a new word from this list to your writing every two to three minutes.

2. Which is a more romantic setting: the beach or a Parisian café? Why?

3. Write about two people who have fallen in love with each other—but they speak two different languages.

4. What is more important in a relationship—words or actions? Why?

5. Argue this point: Love at first sight exists because . . .

6. A romantic meal must include these five things.

7. Who is the couple you know that will stay together forever? What's their secret?

8. He knew she was leaving the country the next day. Here's what happened.

9. The worst anniversary date imaginable is . . .

10. Write about a doomed romance.

11. Reimagine Cupid for the twenty-first century. Be sure to talk about his or her clothing, attitude, and objective in our modern times.

12. Write about the time the wingman got the girl.

13. This is the crazy way she proposed to him.

14. A new law requires you to get married in the next week. Who do you choose to be your partner? Why?

15. Can animals fall in love?

16. They thought they would be together forever, until . . .

17. Describe the wedding day of an arranged marriage. Bonus: Write a scene with this couple 10 years later.

18. Who is your character's strange crush?

19. Here's what the best Valentine's Day looks like. Bonus: Describe the worst Valentine's Day.

20. Is everyone deserving of love? What are the exceptions?

21. The worst pickup line she had ever heard was . . .

22. Two total opposite kinds of people are stuck in an airport together for 24 hours. Here's what happens.

23. Pick an unlikely setting for romance and write about it, like a library, underwater at the pool, or a funeral.

24. Activity: Make a collage of all the things your character loves. Now write a story about a time when they lose one of these things. Bonus: Try another story in which your character loses something else they love.

PROMPT # _____

PROMPT # _____

PROMPT # _____

PROMPT # _____

PROMPT # _____

PROMPT # _____

PROMPT # _____

PROMPT # _____

PROMPT # _____

PORTRAIT OF A PERSON, PLACE, OR THING

Paint a portrait with the following people, places, or things in just three minutes each.

Your Turn

Pick one of these words or phrases and see if sparks fly.

A stolen kiss

Unrequited

A zombie love affair

Where to elope

An unexpected date

PDA gone wrong

What he doesn't know about her

No one falls in love in this town

BONUS

Set your writing from each of these prompts in a different time in history. For instance, you might explore PDA gone wrong in 1908 or an unexpected date in the far future.

BREAK THE LOGJAM

Getting stuck when writing is pretty common—but just because all writers experience it doesn't mean writer's block isn't frustrating. Thankfully, there are lots of ways out of the mire. Try one or two of these tips the next time you're not sure where to go with your writing.

- Write a list of all the possible places the story could go—good, bad, or ridiculous. Pick your top three options and sketch out how the story might unfold. Then pick your favorite of those sketches to break through that writer's block.

- Borrow from a famous book. For example, think about Shakespeare's tragedy *Romeo and Juliet.* You could write your own version of the famous balcony scene but set it in a modern condo or Al Capone's crime-ridden Chicago of the 1920s. You pick the time and setting for your star-crossed lovers. How are they at odds with their era and place in the world, just as Shakespeare's characters were?

- Similarly, take a piece of paper and sit by the television. Flip through the channels and write down the conflicts you see. Ask yourself how your characters would react if they got themselves into comparable situations.

- Use a prompt! You have a whole book of them here. Try outside your genre, too—maybe one of the romance prompts can actually get you unstuck in your sci-fi story in chapter 5: Your Guide to the Galaxy (page 97). Maybe getting creative with a little verse in chapter 6: The Poetry Plunge (page 120) can free you up to write your memoir more effectively.

CHAPTER 5

Your Guide to the Galaxy

Robots, aliens, *Game of Thrones*—whatever your nerdy pleasure, fire up your pen because it's time to spin some fantasy and sci-fi tales. In this chapter, we're going to make use of a setting worksheet to create new worlds and try different characters and conflicts. Then we'll dive into some prompts that could bring your weirdest, most wonderful creations to life.

SETTING WORKSHEET

Name of place:	Type of place (planet, city, kingdom, etc.):
History:	Inhabitants:
Buildings:	Terrain:
Weather:	Transportation:
Time in history:	Time of year:
Time of day:	Mood:

STORY STARTS, GAMES, AND OTHER PROMPTS

Here are some writing games to get your sci-fi gears turning. Remember, you may use the setting from the worksheet on page 98 to build out these story starts.

Your Turn

Pick one of these prompts and go anywhere, anytime.

1. In the year 2552, _____ is illegal now because _____.

2. Start a story that begins with one of these words: epic, challenge, imagine, helium, creature, myth. Bonus: Keep adding a new word from this list to your writing every two to three minutes.

3. In this isolated village, people only have one of three jobs. What are they?

4. Describe a place where mermaids live.

5. There is a species of human that lives above the clouds. This is what they look like and why they live there.

6. A(n) _____ has unexpectedly come to life. This is what it tells you.

7. Build an animal that lives on another planet. Describe what it eats, where it sleeps, and what makes it angry.

8. A witch who has recently lost her powers encounters an evil archenemy.

9. Look up what the musical instrument known as a "theremin" sounds like. Write for three minutes with this instrument as your prompt.

10. In the new world, everyone drinks the same morning elixir. What does it taste like? What is its purpose?

11. You come home one day and your dad is making dinner. He smiles quizzically and asks, "Who are you?"

12. Start a story that begins with one of these words: gravity, spacious, barren, orbiting, crater. Bonus: Keep adding a new word from this list to your writing every two to three minutes.

13. Cars have become obsolete. This is the new way people travel.

14. A medicine has been developed that cures _____. But it has a controversial ingredient. Write about the medicine and the controversy surrounding it.

15. Recently, a genetic mutation has been discovered. Those with the mutation are able to _____.

16. In 1,000 years, textiles are totally different than they are today. Write about what clothes feel like in the future.

17. It's been discovered that we can interpret animals' brainwaves and determine our pets' thoughts. Write about the findings.

18. You predict _____ and it comes true. Here's what happens after.

19. Scientists have built a device that can go back in time. It has been found that the device's best use is to change parts of history. Pick five places in the past you'd go and what you would change.

PROMPT # _____

PROMPT # _____

PROMPT # _____

PROMPT # _____

PROMPT # _____

PROMPT # _____

PROMPT # _____

PROMPT # _____

PROMPT # _____

PROMPT # _____

PORTRAIT OF A PERSON, PLACE, OR THING

Paint a speedy word portrait by limiting yourself to only three minutes to write about the following person, place, or thing. (You can always come back to this later and use your quick write as the basis for your first novel.)

Your Turn

Choose a phrase and take off to places unknown.

How the nanobot feels	A device that can stop the aging process
A child heir in a faraway land	The last settlers on our planet

A dream traveler

A shape-shifter

A newly uncovered underground creature

The truth about the pandemic

ADD A PLOT TWIST

Choose one of these when you want to introduce a new sidekick character or deepen the plot of one of the stories started in the preceding section.

Your Turn

Grab a prompt, a jet propulsion system, the sword from the stone, or whatever else you'll need to survive in a new reality.

1. Your character learns that she has been under surveillance throughout her entire journey.

2. He's been exposed to a virus—from another planet.

3. Every night, your character sees a flashing light that seems to come from a distant field.

4. Your character breaks into a top-secret government lab to find . . .

5. Your character receives a note under his door that reads, "Leave immediately."

6. A highly advanced remote control arrives in the mail with strangely written instructions for how to use it.

7. Your character passes a woman in an alley who looks exactly like her.

8. The village elder has vanished without a trace.

9. A friend calls unexpectedly . . . to say she has finally contacted alien life forms.

PROMPT # _____

PROMPT # _____

PROMPT # _____

PROMPT # _____

PROMPT # _____

TAKE TWO

Read over anything you've written lately. We're on the lookout for clichés, phrases that are so overused in writing that they have gotten stale or lost their meaning.

Here are some examples:

- It was a dark and stormy night.
- Leave no stone unturned.
- She had a heart of gold.
- Only time will tell.
- They lived happily ever after.

Certain phrases may be overused, but they befit the occasion they are used for. Here are a couple that are not considered clichés:

- Happy birthday!
- I now pronounce you husband and wife.

The problem with clichés, though, is that they are so common that sometimes we use them without even realizing it. This is why revision is such an important part of the writing process because, among other things, it gives us a chance to go back and scan for overused phrases.

Go through your text and try to spot any words or ideas that are clichéd and make fresh choices. Once you've completed a self-edit, turn over your story to someone else for a second look, and maybe even a general critique. There is more on asking for feedback in *Share Your Work* in chapter 7 (page 145).

CHAPTER 6

The Poetry Plunge

Poetry is the less-is-more genre of writing where every word counts. But poems aren't just meant to be brief; they also do a lot of work with very little. They teach you that rhyme, rhythm, and metaphor are great ways to capture your reader's attention. Tapping into an image, gesture, action, mood, or complex emotion can inspire memorable poems. Go ahead, write about the things that move you.

WAIT, THAT'S A POEM?

As you've probably seen, poems come in many different styles. I penned these three examples to inspire you to write poetry *your* way.

Don't speak of always.
Show it to me.

You were wearing wool that day,
a thick protective layer,
—snug around your heart.

One, two, three—
the intervals between brilliant breaks of light across night sky—
accompany whistling wind
and transport us to the back porch to watch.
Her tired frown brings me tea
and my small hand intertwines hers
for a moment . . . just.
And as she rocks,
in her creaking, rust-ingrained, old porch chair,
slowly, then recklessly,
I stare . . .
first at the storm
then at her story
that she keeps,
swings, surreptitiously,
Back and forth,
away from me.

TOPIC PROMPTS

I understand that starting on your own poems might not be as easy as it sounds, so go ahead and borrow a phrase or word from the lines below to jump-start your poetry writing.

Your Turn

Let's see where these words take you.

1. A jagged tooth stuck in the tree
2. The tallest flowers she had ever seen
3. The tower crumbled
4. Pulsation
5. Emerge
6. Flying
7. A forbidden calling
8. Summer storms
9. Lost in the everyday
10. Reckless
11. Cavern
12. A remembered thought
13. Frenemies
14. An amethyst
15. Distant emotions
16. A misunderstood demon
17. Bleak aftermath
18. A tattered dress
19. It's a sign
20. Wonder
21. Homes with no doors
22. The fragrant fireworks
23. Her unsolicited advice
24. Endless echoes
25. The garbage goes unnoticed
26. Elbows all askew
27. Creative curfews
28. Patience
29. The faded page
30. Fuzzy musical madness
31. Blazing rage
32. Fruit trees
33. An alias
34. Beginner's luck
35. Heated secret
36. Busted phone
37. Rattle
38. Impromptu party
39. Puzzled
40. Noiselessness

PROMPT # _____

PROMPT # _____

PROMPT # _____

PROMPT # _____

PROMPT # _____

PROMPT # _____

PROMPT # _____

PROMPT # _____

PROMPT # _____

PROMPT # _____

HAIKU YOU?

Haiku is a poem that originated in Japan in the 1600s. A haiku contains three lines and a particular number of syllables—five in the first line, seven in the second, five in the third.

Usually haiku juxtapose two ideas and contain a seasonal reference, but really, you can use the structure to write about any topic that interests you!

FOR EXAMPLE

Here's my take on haiku—to show you that your poems can be as Zen or as zany as you want.

The blue winter comes
Quickly, angrily, steadfast
Reminder of time.

Sound of tornadoes,
Pots, pans crashing together,
Cats . . . mating season.

Us, connected, one
Soon, you chose a new girlfriend . . .
Too bad that she smells.

Don't pooh-pooh the haiku. You might think following rules about syllables will quash your creativity. On the contrary. Constraints often feed the imaginative juices, pushing your clever mind in fresh new directions. Here are a few syllables to help you take off.

Your Turn

All right. Now it's up to you. The prompts here should get your haiku cooing.

1. Lightning
2. Curious
3. Blessing
4. Ember
5. Forget
6. Kiss
7. Captivate
8. Rain
9. Obstacle
10. Abyss

11. Delicious
12. Expedition
13. Winter
14. Daydream
15. Exception
16. Melody
17. Harlot
18. Decadence
19. Vacation
20. Midnight

DOUBLE WHAMMY CHALLENGE:

Take a prompt phrase you already used and write a whole new poem with it.

PROMPT # _____

PROMPT # _____

PROMPT # _____

PROMPT # _____

PROMPT # _____

PROMPT # _____

PROMPT # _____

PROMPT # _____

PROMPT # _____

PROMPT # _____

CHAPTER 7

Keep on Truckin'

Good-bye already? Almost, but not quite! Here, I properly bid you adieu by giving some helpful suggestions, resources, and words of encouragement as you continue your writing journey.

THANKS FOR PLAYING

I hope you've had fun uncovering your beliefs and opinions and unleashing new worlds, characters, and ideas through these writing prompts. Remember that you can always come back to *Dare to Write* to expand on stories or write completely new ones. Here are some things to keep in mind as you continue:

- Just like a good athlete makes time to sleep, eat well, and exercise, a good writer seeks out new experiences to influence their writing.

- Writers learn from the pros—they take classes and listen to other writers online, in person, or wherever they can.

- Writers find a creative community. They seek out like-minded souls who encourage each other. Writing can be lonely. But it doesn't have to be!

- Writers read a lot.

- Most importantly perhaps, all the best writing instructors have taught me that writers . . . write. Writers don't have to create masterpieces every time—in fact, they rarely write anything resembling a masterpiece the first time. But they develop a writing practice and consistently carve out time for it.

COOL RESOURCES AND RECOMMENDED READING FOR ASPIRING WRITERS

Here are a few online resources to aid in the writing process:

- Search "prompt generator" online to get randomly selected first lines, plot twists, even genre and character bonding moment generators.

- Create a new board on Pinterest with all the writing ideas you find. You can also discover a ton of inspiring aspiring writers on Instagram.

- If you're stuck with a grammar or nuts-and-bolts writing question, Purdue's Online Writing Lab and Grammar Girl are two of my favorite resources.

And check out these game-changing resources in book form:

- *Writing Down the Bones* by Natalie Goldberg—a must-have for rock-solid tips on the craft of writing and the writing practice from an acclaimed author.

- *The Artist's Way* by Julia Cameron—a life-changing book that will get any writer unstuck; her morning pages process alone will improve your writing almost instantly.

- *A Writer's Book of Days* by Judy Reeves—a treasure trove of practical suggestions, expert advice, powerful inspiration, and a ton of prompts.

SHARE YOUR WORK

Sharing your work can be an inspiring—or intimidating—part of your writing life. If you've written something you really enjoy but can't totally assess it objectively, a fresh set of eyes can tell you if the plot is confusing or if a character seems more evil than you had intended, for example. Sometimes what we think is on the page, isn't quite there yet.

But beware! Stories sometimes die at this stage because writers don't always share their work with the right person. Choose someone who will be honest, but also gentle and supportive—preferably someone who reads a lot and cares about stories. Then reflect on their advice, deciding for yourself what's truly useful.

Good people to share your work with:

- a teacher you respect
- a friend who enjoys reading and writing as well
- other practicing writers who know what it's like to work on stories
- a parent who encourages you
- a local author you admire who encourages new writers

When you reach out for advice, it's always helpful to ask for something specific. "Please let me know how realistic the dialogue is for these characters in this time period" is a more helpful than "Read this and tell me what you think."

Lastly, remember to take any feedback you receive with a grain of salt. You control your story. So if you really believe in it and others don't, that's fine. Keep at it, because you are the author.

Dialogue Bonus Round

Let's find a voice. Imagine two very different characters and how they would express themselves if they wanted to quit their jobs and completely overhaul their lives:

- A present-day, brash New York City homicide detective

- A proper fifteenth century queen

In a few sentences, let both of them announce the news. For example, the queen might inform her kingdom that she'd rather be a hairdresser or an explorer. Experiment with the detective telling his news to other cops or on live TV. Have fun.

Give it a go

Go on

EXTRA, EXTRA, WRITE ALL ABOUT IT—

Not so fast! This prompt book ain't over till it's over. Here are some bonus prompts from every writing genre we covered in *Dare to Write*. You know what to do.

1. An interrupted routine
2. The color of laughter
3. The unopened piece of mail
4. Playing favorites
5. My mother's decision
6. Packed and ready to go
7. Whirlwind
8. Best day ever . . . almost
9. It wasn't a game
10. An interview
11. The speeding ticket
12. The ripped shirt
13. The lost ID
14. Piano music
15. I learned the hard way
16. With shaky hands
17. The teachers' lounge
18. Revenge
19. Her dreams
20. Lightly falling snow
21. Something smells
22. A million dollars
23. 6:24 a.m.
24. The skyline in a new city
25. Motionless
26. The witness protection program
27. A tumbleweed
28. At the festival
29. A caution sign
30. Haters
31. Risking it all
32. I wasn't who they thought
33. The expert in her field
34. Luck
35. Before internet
36. The day the internet vanished
37. Skeletons
38. A lake cabin
39. A comical disaster
40. Second place
41. A fall from power
42. A tarot card reader
43. A significant acquaintance
44. Inside out
45. Luxury
46. An artifact
47. What $5 gets you
48. Karma
49. Cartwheeling
50. The necessary lie
51. The opened cage
52. The briefcase with a broken lock
53. My application for space station manager
54. My resignation from the frozen yogurt shop

PROMPT # _____

PROMPT # _____

PROMPT # _____

PROMPT # _____

PROMPT # _____

PROMPT # _____

PROMPT # _____

PROMPT # _____

PROMPT # _____

PROMPT # _____

PROMPT # _____

PROMPT # _____

PROMPT # _____

PROMPT # _____

PROMPT # _____

Acknowledgments

For Mom, Joey, and Declan, as well as a big thank-you to my family and friends, the best characters I know.

Everyone at Callisto—particularly Vanessa and Rochelle—I appreciate your guidance and feedback.

Lastly, I'm ever so grateful to be a part of San Diego Writers, Ink. I continually learn how to be a little more daring with *my* words from these gifted writers, instructors, and creatives.

About the Author

Kristen Fogle is a former magazine editor who has interviewed celebrities such as Taylor Swift and the Kardashians. Since 2013 she has been the executive director of San Diego Writers, Ink, as well as a writing instructor, teaching artist, and theatrical producer, director, and performer. You can find out more about her classes and productions at KristenFogle.com or SanDiegoWriters.org.